BE CREATIVE

Accessories
for All

Anna Claybourne

A+
Smart Apple Media

Published by Smart Apple Media, an imprint of Black Rabbit Books
P.O. Box 3263, Mankato, Minnesota 56002
www.blackrabbitbooks.com

Printed in the United States of America at Corporate Graphics, North Mankato, Minnesota.

Published by arrangement with the Watts Publishing Group LTD, London.

Library of Congress Cataloging-in-Publication Data
Claybourne, Anna.
 Accessories for all / Anna Claybourne.
    p. cm. -- (Be creative)
 Includes index.
 Summary: "Using clear, illustrated step-by-step directions, these books explain how to create funky accessories with little bits of fabric, ribbon, buttons, and more. Basic sewing skills are taught, and ideas for other crafts are prompted. Equipment resources and glossary are included"--Provided by publisher.
 ISBN 978-1-59920-694-3 (library binding)
 1. Dress accessories--Juvenile literature. I. Title.
 TT649.8.C53 2013
 391.4'4--dc23

                                              2011039545

Produced for Franklin Watts by White-Thomson Publishing

Author: **Anna Claybourne**
Project manager: **Rachel Minay**
Creative director: **Simon Balley**
Design: **Balley Design Limited**
Designer/Illustrator: **Andrew Li**

Picture Credits
Shutterstock: Africa Studio front cover/3/4/10/19/23/27/28/30/32, akiyoko 2/4/7/10/14/27/31/32/back cover, Alexandr Makarov 21, Andrea Haase 16/17, Andrea Slatter 17, Arkady Mazor 24/25/30–31, bociek666 5/9, Chris Leachman 12, Elena Elisseeva front cover/9/27, Fedorov Oleksiy 7, Flashon Studio 25, Gaby Kooijman 25, Hank Frentz 28/29, Ingrid Prats front cover/2/4/6/7, Irina Rubanova 4, jackhollingsworthcom LLC 5, Jason Stitt 21, 23, Jiri Hera 28/29, Kabakova Tatyana 16/17, karnizz 15, Kayros Studio "Be Happy!" 26/27, Kimberly Hall 2/5/18/22/31/32, Konstantin Yolshin 13, Iantapix 17, Mauro Rodrigues 7, Maxim Godkin 29, Picsfive 27/29, Rafa Irusta 21, Rago Arts 13, Razvy 4/9/10/11/17, Rene Jansa 23, Sergey Goruppa 8/9, Shmeliova Natalia 3, Silvia Bukovac 7, Stormur 26, Tamara Kulikova 4/5/8, Tim Arbaev 11, Tom Prokop 15, vblinov 14/15/back cover, Yuri Arcurs 7, ZoneFatal front cover/2/6/12.

Note: Every effort has been made by the publishers to ensure that the websites on page 30 of this book are suitable for children and that they contain no inappropriate or offensive material. However, because of the nature of the Internet, it is impossible to guarantee that the contents of these sites will not be altered. We strongly advise that Internet access is supervised by a responsible adult.

PO1435
2-2012

9 8 7 6 5 4 3 2 1

Contents

Words in **bold** are in the glossary on page 31.

All about Accessories

Accessories are all the extra things that go with your clothes, such as bags, hats, and jewelry. They can liven up an outfit and show off your own style. It's fun and creative to make your own—and it saves money!

Get the Gear!

For the projects in this book, you'll need basic sewing needles, pins, buttons, thread and scissors, which you may have at home. For jewelry-making, you need cord, beads, metal **findings** (such as necklace **clasps**), and jewelry **pliers**, which you can get at craft and bead shops. Any small, fine-tipped pliers from home would work too.

Do It Yourself (DIY)

Making your own accessories means you can have funky stuff whenever you want. It's far cheaper than buying them new, and it's simple and fun to do. You could even end up with a career as a jeweler or fashion designer!

Safety

Remember to keep strings, cords, and sharp things like pins, needles, and scissors away from small children.

Tip!
If you have a sewing machine and know how it works, you can use it for some of the projects in this book.

Use It Again
Crafting is green too, because old things can be repaired or recycled rather than thrown into a **landfill**. You can make some accessories out of old clothes or junk, or mend and rework old things so that you can use them again.

In the Box
Keep all your creative stuff together in a craft box. You can buy one or make your own with a shoebox.

5

Perfect Pendant

A simple **pendant** is one of the easiest and quickest accessories you can make. String it together, put it on, and away you go! This is also a great way to reuse broken pieces of jewelry.

Get the Gear!

- About 3 feet (1 m) of cotton jewelry cord
- Bead, shell, or whatever you are using for the pendant
- Necklace clasp (see box on page 7)
- Scissors

1

String your bead or other item onto the middle of the cord. Tie a double knot to hold it in place.

2

Hold the cord around your neck to decide how long to make it. Cut to the right length, leaving about 4 in. (10 cm) extra on each end.

Tip!
Always make sure your beads have holes big enough for your cord to go through.

Necklace Clasps

There are various types of necklace clasps:

  (1) ring and hook

  (2) ring and bar (or a toggle)

  (3) spring ring

You can attach them all by tying them on.

❶

❷

❸

3 Tie the two ends of cord tightly to the two parts of the clasp using double knots. Trim off any extra cord.

Tip!
Go beachcombing! A pebble or shell with a hole in it will make a great pendant.

Knotted Cord Necklace

This is a quick and easy way to make a necklace or bracelet, but it looks really professional.

Get the Gear!

- 3–6 ft. (1–2 m) of cotton jewelry cord
- Selection of beads
- Necklace clasp
- Pliers and scissors

1

Beads come in lots of styles, sizes, and colors, so think about what color scheme or pattern you want to use. Lay your cord down and try out different arrangements before you start.

Tip!
If your design is complicated, draw a sketch of it to work from.

2

To put a bead onto the cord, tie a knot bigger than the bead hole, thread the bead on, and tie another knot on the other side. Start in the middle of the cord and work your way to the ends. You can space out the beads however you like.

Patterns

Try arranging the beads and cord to make different patterns like these:

3

Some beads have big holes that will slip over a knot. For these, thread the cord through the bead, tie a knot and thread through again, like this. The knot will end up inside the bead.

4

Finally, trim the cord to the right length and add the clasp (see page 7). If you want a long necklace, you can just knot it and pop it over your head. Make a shorter version if you want a bracelet.

Button Jewelry

Buttons come in all colors, shapes, and sizes and don't cost much. They're perfect for threading onto cord to make necklaces and bracelets.

Get the Gear!

- 3–6 ft. (1–2 m) of cotton jewelry cord
- Scissors
- Buttons
- Necklace clasps

Tip!
Some buttons have two holes, some have four, and some have one hole at the back. Experiment with different ways of threading them.

Button Bead Necklace

You can simply use buttons instead of beads, or mix them with beads for a quirky necklace. Thread the cord through two holes in the button, like this. If your buttons slip along the cord, tie a knot at the back of each one.

Button Bangle

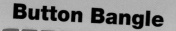

1 This is a great way to use up lots of spare buttons. Use strong jewelry cord or elastic, knot one end, and thread buttons onto it tightly packed together. You only need to use one of the holes in each button.

2 When it's long enough, tie a knot at the other end, and attach a clasp (see page 7). Or tie the ends together to make a slip-on bracelet (check the size first).

Tip!
Look for buttons in bargain bins at sewing shops, rummage sales, and thrift stores. Keep a button collection in a jar or tin, so you'll always have buttons to use.

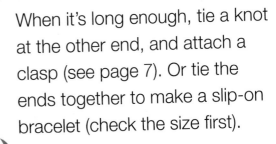

Charm Bracelet

A charm bracelet is a chunky chain bracelet with little "charms" hanging from it. Charms can be little jewelry shapes, buttons, beads, or whatever you like. Some bead shops sell charm bracelet chains ready to use, or you can make one from a short length of chain.

Get the Gear!

- About 12 in. (30 cm) of open-link chain (from a bead shop or from old jewelry)
- 10–20 **jump rings** (small metal rings)
- Up to 10 charms or jewelry shapes with holes
- Pliers
- Necklace clasp

1 Measure how long your bracelet should be to fit around your wrist loosely. To shorten the chain, use pliers to open one of the links and remove as many as necessary.

2 Add a clasp (see page 7), using pliers to open and close the chain links.

Tip!
If you can't open the chain links, attach the clasp using jump rings (see step 3).

3 To add each charm, use a jump ring. Use your pliers to open the ring by gripping one side of the ring tightly in the pliers, and pushing the other side with your fingers. Then thread the ring through the hole in your charm, and through a link in the chain. Close the ring again with the pliers.

Style ideas

1 Use alphabet letters to spell a name or word.

2 Choose charms that fit a theme, such as moons and stars, or flowers.

3 Use charms that are all the same color.

Tip!
If you can't find an open-link chain, use an 8 in. (20 cm) piece of sewing elastic instead. Thread lots of jump rings all the way along it, then tie into a loop and trim the ends.

Felt Hair Clips

These hair clips are easy to make and easy to wear. Express yourself by creating any shape or picture you like! You can mix them up and wear a different one every day.

Get the Gear!

- Pencil, paper, and pen
- Simple metal hairclips
- 2 or 3 squares of felt in different colors
- Sewing thread
- Beads, buttons, or **sequins**

1 First, draw your design onto paper, making it about the same size as a hair clip. For your first attempt, try a simple shape like a heart. Add a smaller shape inside.

2 Copy your shape outline onto a piece of felt twice using a pen, and cut out both pieces (they will be the front and back). Draw and cut out the smaller shape in a different color. Then pin the small shape on top of one of the larger pieces.

3 Sew the shapes together using a **running stitch** (see box on page 15). Remove the pins. You can also sew on beads or other decorations (see box on page 17).

Take the back piece, fold it in half and make two small cuts, like this (2). Then open it up and it will have two slits cut in it (3). Line it up with the front part, and sew the two together with running stitch all around (4).

1 **2**

3 **4**

Finally take your hair clip and slide it through the slits at the back to attach it.

How to Do a Running Stitch

A running stitch is a very simple stitch where you simply sew in and out of the fabric in a straight line. It is most useful for sewing thick fabrics, **gathering** fabrics, or to make a decorative stitch.

Tip!
More design ideas for hair clips:

Airplane
Apple
Bee
Butterfly

Flower
Cupcake
Face
Rainbow

Flower Brooch

A funky flower to pin to your favorite coat—or make one for your grandma as a present!

Get the Gear!

- Pencil, paper, and pen
- A pack of felt squares in different colors
- Scissors, pins, and needles
- Sewing thread in different colors
- Small beads, buttons, or sequins
- Safety pin

1 Start by sketching some flower shapes. The brooch should have a large flower outline and up to three smaller shapes inside, with a button or bead in the middle.

2 Copy your shapes onto different colors of felt with a pen, and cut them out. Arrange them on top of each other and pin together.

Sewing on Beads and Buttons

To sew on the decorations, knot your thread, sew through from the back of the brooch, and thread the needle through the holes in the button or bead. Then sew through to the back again. Repeat several times before knotting at the back.

3

Sew around each smaller shape with a running stitch (see page 15), sewing through all the layers. Remove the pins. If you like, sew beads, buttons, or sequins in the middle (see box above).

4

Now sew the safety pin to the back. Knot the thread and push the needle through the bottom layer of felt, just below the side of the pin that doesn't open. Pull the thread back toward you over the top of the pin. Sew over and over to make it secure before knotting in the back.

Sew a Simple Scarf

A scarf is a great way to dress up an outfit, but they can cost a lot at the store! Yet a scarf is just a piece of fabric with the edges sewn. If you make your own, you can have scarves in any fabric you like—and it's a great way to get started with sewing.

Get the Gear!

- Fabric (see Tip box on page 19)
- Tape measure, scissors, pins, and needles
- Thread to match your fabric

1 You can make your scarf any shape, but a rectangle is easiest to start with. A good size is about 36 in. x 12 in. (90 cm x 30 cm). Cut your fabric to the right size, adding 1 in. (2 cm) all around for the **hem** (folded-over edge).

2 To hem the scarf, fold in each edge by ½ in. (1 cm) and then by ½ in. (1 cm) again, so the **raw edge** is hidden inside. Do the two sides first, then the two ends, so that the corners are neatly tucked in. Pin the hem in place.

½ in. (1 cm)

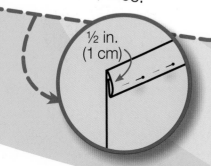

36 in. (90 cm)

12 in. (30 cm)

1 in. (2 cm)

3

Thread your needle with a piece of thread about 24 in. (60 cm) long, and knot the end. Sew around the scarf using a **backstitch** (see box below), removing the pins as you go. When you get to the end of the thread, knot it, trim the end, and thread some more. You can use a sewing machine if you have one.

Tip!
Cotton, silk, and linen are good fabrics for scarves. Lightweight cotton is easiest to sew. Silky or stretchy fabrics are harder. You can buy new fabric at a fabric store, or reuse old clothes.

How to Do a Backstitch

1 Push the needle tip in and out of the fabric, making a small stitch.

2 Go back to where the thread disappears into the fabric and push the needle in.

3 Push the needle up, coming out a little farther along.

4 Do the same with each stitch, going back to fill in the space left by the stitch before.

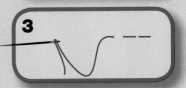

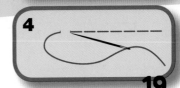

Sweater Scarf

When your favorite sweater gets a few holes or doesn't fit any more, you can make it into a cozy winter scarf.

Get the Gear!

- Old sweater
- Scissors, pins, and needles
- Tape measure or ruler
- Extra-strong sewing thread

1 The easiest way to make a scarf is from the sweater's sleeves. First, cut off both sleeves neatly, as high up as possible.

2 Turn one sleeve inside out and pull it over the other arm, so that the ends line up. Then pin around the cut end, about 1 in. (2 cm) from the edge.

3 Sew around the ends, using a backstitch (see page 19), removing the pins as you go.

Turn it right side out and you'll have a long scarf! You can wear it like this, or sew the ends closed first if you prefer.

Tip!
Knitted wool is quite thick, so make sure you stick the needle through both layers. You need to pin and sew at least 1 in. (2 cm) from the edge, because the edge may start to unravel after you cut it.

4

Tip!
Another way to make a scarf is to cut the feet off old, worn-out socks, and sew the leg parts together.

Sweater Stocking Hat

An old sweater can also be turned into a cozy winter hat. If you haven't already done so, you could make a matching scarf (see pages 20–21).

Get the Gear!

- Old sweater
- Tape measure, scissors, pins, and needles
- Extra-strong sewing thread
- Yarn and cardboard for pom-pom, if needed

1 Measure the **circumference** of your head (the distance all the way around it). Divide by 2 to find the width you need.

2 Turn the sweater inside out, and lay it flat with the bottom edges lined up. Use pins to make a rounded hat shape with the right width. Make the height about the same as the width.

3 Cut out the hat, leaving about 1 in. (2 cm) extra around the pins.

4

Sew along the pin line using a backstitch (see page 19), removing the pins as you go. Turn it right side out and your hat is ready!

Add a Pom-pom

Cut two rings of cardboard like this, and hold them together.

1¼ in. (3 cm)

3 in. (8 cm)

Wind yarn around and around the rings until you can't fit any more through the middle. Use scissors to cut between the two cardboard rings and cut through all the yarn.

Wind a piece of yarn around the bundle, between the cardboard rings. Pull it tight and knot it to hold it in place.

Pull the cardboard rings off and there's your pom-pom! Sew it to the top of your hat.

Drawstring Bag

This simple bag can be whatever you want it to be. With tough fabric it could be a gym bag, or make a softer version to keep your PJs in. Or you can make a mini one for coins or jewelry.

Get the Gear!

- Fabric (cotton is easiest to sew)
- Tape measure, scissors, pins, and needles
- Thread to match your fabric
- Curtain cord, bias tape, or ribbon for the drawstring
- Safety pin

1 Decide on a size for your bag. A PJ bag could be about 12 in. x 8 in. (30 cm x 20 cm). Cut a piece of fabric twice as wide as your bag will be (e.g. 8 in. x 2 = 16 in. (40 cm) and as high as your bag, plus an extra 2 in. (5 cm) all around.

2 Fold the fabric in half "right sides together." This means that the "right" side (the patterned side or the "best" side) is facing inward and the "wrong" side is facing outward. Pin along the bottom and side.

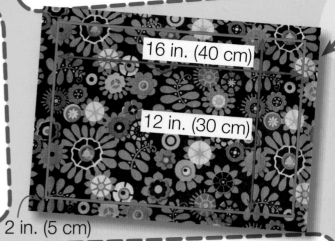

16 in. (40 cm)

12 in. (30 cm)

2 in. (5 cm)

2 in. (5 cm)

3 Then thread your needle and sew firmly along the bottom and side using a backstitch (see page 19) or a sewing machine. Remove the pins. Leave 2 in. (5 cm) open at the top of the side.

4 Fold back the raw edges of the opening on each side and sew them down to make a neat edge.

5 Fold the top edge of the bag over twice, all the way around. Pin close to the edge (the gap above will need to be big enough for your cord or ribbon). Sew using a backstitch, removing the pins as you go.

6 Attach the cord or ribbon to a safety pin to make it easier to thread through the top edge of your bag. Then tie it at the end to make a loop. Turn your bag right side out.

Tip!
A gym bag should be about 16 in. x 12 in. (40 cm x 30 cm), so you would need a piece of fabric 24 in. (60 cm) wide and 16 in. (40 cm) high plus 2 in. (5 cm) all around.

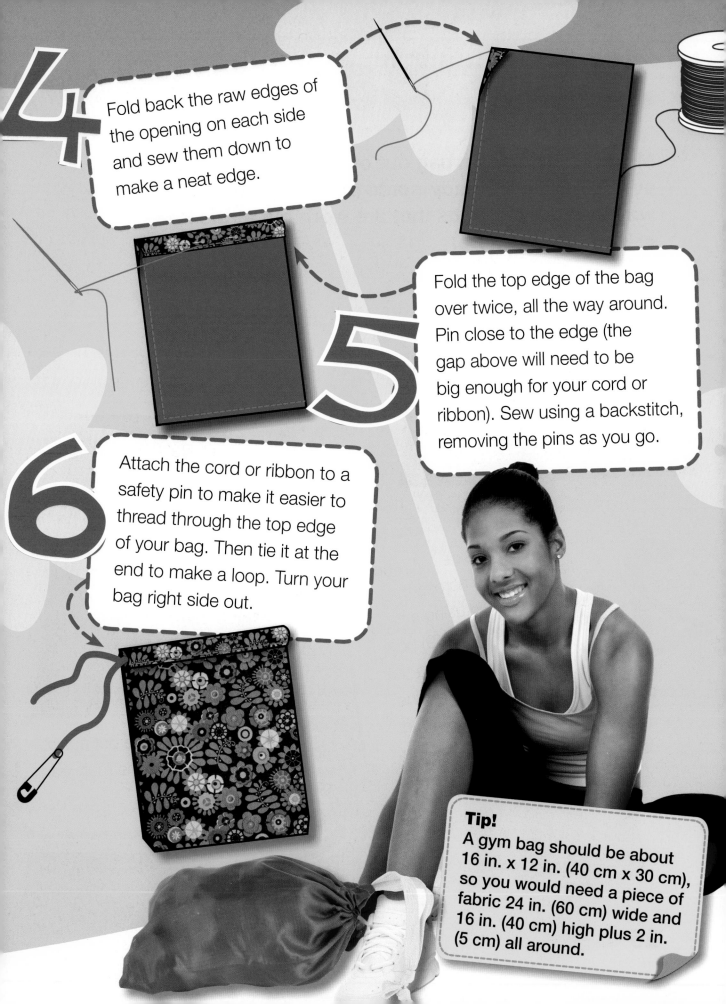

Jeans Bag

Make a funky denim bag out of an old pair of jeans—it even comes with ready-made pockets! This is a great way to reuse old jeans that are worn out at the knee or don't fit any more.

Get the Gear!

- Old jeans
- Tape measure, scissors, pins, and needles
- Extra-strong sewing thread

1 Lay the jeans flat and cut off the legs across the top. Keep one leg to make the strap.

2 Turn the jeans inside out, and lay flat again. Pin across the bottom, then sew using a backstitch (see page 19) or a sewing machine. Remove the pins. Sew over the same line twice to make it really strong.

3 Turn right side out again. And there's the main part of your bag!

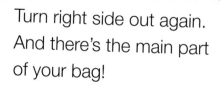

4 To make the strap, cut a strip of fabric from one leg about 4 in. (10 cm) wide and 20 in. (50 cm) long (or longer or shorter, depending on how long you want the strap).

5 Fold the strip in half, and fold the edges in. Pin along the edge, then sew using a backstitch or a sewing machine. Remove the pins.

6 Lastly, sew the strap to the bag. Fold the ends of the strap over and pin to the inside of the bag at the sides. Then sew both ends on firmly, sewing in a square to make it strong.

Tip!
If you want to be able to close your bag, sew on two short pieces of ribbon in the middle so you can tie the sides together.

You could sew on beads or buttons to decorate your bag.

Crafty Roll-up

This roll-up holder is great for carrying your craft supplies when you're on the go. You could also use it to hold makeup and hair products or pens and pencils.

Get the Gear!

- 2 pieces of fabric about 8 in. x 12 in. (20 cm x 30 cm)
- About 1 yd. (1 m) of elastic that is ¼–½ in. (1–2 cm) wide
- Tape measure, scissors, pins, and needles
- Sewing thread
- About 10 in. (25 cm) of ribbon

1 Cut out your fabric pieces, allowing an extra 1 in. (2 cm) all around.

12 in. (30 cm)

8 in. (20 cm)

extra 1 in. (2 cm)

2 Cut your elastic into two strips about 16 in. (40 cm) long each. Fold over one end of elastic and pin it to one piece of fabric at one end. Then pin the elastic to the fabric in a series of loops. Small loops could hold scissors, bigger loops could hold spools of thread. Fold over the other end of the elastic and pin down.

3 Pin another piece of elastic on the same way. Use a backstitch (see page 19) to sew the elastic on, and remove the pins.

4

Now lay the elastic-covered fabric down, and lay the other piece of fabric on top, "right" sides (see page 24) together.

4 in. (10 cm) gap

5

Pin and sew around the edges using a backstitch, leaving a 4 in. (10 cm) gap at one side. Remove the pins.

6

Turn the holder right side out and sew along the gap. Fold the ribbon in half and sew it onto one edge of the holder, like this. Once you've filled your roll with all your supplies, roll it up and use the ribbon to tie it.

Equipment Tips

Here's a quick guide to finding and using the gear you need for making accessories.

Beads
Craft shops, toy stores, and sewing shops often have beads, and there are also specialty bead shops. You can reuse beads from old or broken jewelry too.

Bias tape
This is like ribbon, but made of fabric. It's used to finish edges of fabric. Find it in sewing shops.

Buttons
You can buy buttons in sewing shops, craft shops, and discount stores. Also try thrift stores and reusing buttons from old clothes.

Cotton jewelry cord
Craft and bead shops sell strong, waxed cotton cord for making necklaces. It comes in lots of colors and is sold by the yard or meter, or in small packs.

Curtain cord
You can get this thick, soft cord at fabric shops and curtain shops.

Elastic
Sewing shops sell elastic by the yard or meter, or in little packs.

Fabric
Fabric shops, craft shops, and some department stores sell new fabrics by the yard or meter. Check bargain bins for cheaper **remnants**. Ask friends and family if they have old clothes, bed linens, or curtains you could cut up and reuse.

Felt
Fabric shops, discount stores, and craft shops often have felt.

Findings
Findings are the metal parts for making jewelry, such as jump rings, necklace clasps, and chains. You'll find them at bead shops and craft shops.

Hair clips
Find them at accessory shops and clothing stores.

Jewelry pliers
Find at craft and bead shops, but any small, fine-tipped pliers from a toolbox will work too.

Needles
Find at sewing and some hardware stores. Look for a variety pack with lots of different sizes.

Old clothes
As well as reusing your own old fabrics, ask family members for anything they don't want any more, and check out thrift stores and rummage sales.

Online
There are many fabric and craft shops on the Internet. You may find the following sites useful starting points:
www.fabric.com
www.amazon.com/Arts-Crafts-Sewing

Pins
Find at sewing shops. Longer pins with ball-shaped heads are the easiest to use.

Ribbons
Sewing and fabric shops usually sell ribbons and trimmings by the yard or meter.

Scissors
Sharp scissors are easiest to work with. Special sewing, craft, or embroidery scissors from a sewing shop are best.

Sequins
You can often find these at craft shops and discount stores.

Sewing machines
This book doesn't show you how to use a sewing machine, but if you have one, you can use it for most of the sewing projects. Follow the machine's instructions, and get an adult to help you. If you want to buy a sewing machine, try a discount store or sewing shop.

Tape measure
Find at sewing shops or discount stores.

Thread
Find at sewing shops, hardware stores, and discount stores. It's worth buying good quality thread as it's easier to sew with. Use extra-strong thread for sewing through heavy or thick fabrics.

Yarn
Find at sewing shops, craft shops, or discount stores.

Glossary

accessories
Bags, scarves, jewelry, and other "extra" parts of an outfit.

backstitch
A strong sewing stitch that goes over each part of the fabric twice.

circumference
The distance all the way around something.

clasp
The part of a necklace or bracelet that holds it closed or opens up.

findings
Metal jewelry parts, such as chains, clips, rings, and clasps.

gather
To pull fabric together into a bundle using a line of stitching.

hem
The edge of a piece of fabric, folded over and sewn in place to stop the fabric from unravelling.

jump ring
A tiny simple metal ring that can be bent to open or close it.

landfill
A place where garbage is buried in the ground.

pendant
A single jewel, shell or other item that hangs on a necklace.

pliers
A tool for holding and gripping objects.

raw edge
The unfinished or cut edge of a piece of fabric.

remnants
Leftover pieces of fabric.

running stitch
A simple, in-and-out sewing stitch.

sequins
Little shiny or metallic discs with a hole in the middle.

Index